"STEVE, I'VE GOT THIS!"

"STEVE, I'VE GOT THIS!"

NOT JUST THE TITLE, BUT THE WORDS JESUS ACTUALLY SPOKE TO ME IN A DREAM.

STEVE HODGES

XULON ELITE

Xulon Press Elite
2301 Lucien Way #415
Maitland, FL 32751
407.339.4217
www.xulonpress.com

Paperback ISBN-13: 978-1-66285-284-8
Ebook ISBN-13: 978-1-66285-285-5

Table of Contents

Dedication

This book is dedicated to my loving wife, June, and to my daughters, Lindy and Melissa, who have helped us in so many ways—by staying at the hospital so June could get some rest, by looking for new hospitals for me to transfer to—and for all their helping June figure out the many bills as they came in. To my sons, Jacob and John, as well as my sons-in-law, Chris and Kiley. Also, a special dedication to my friend Travis Roth, who stepped forward to volunteer to organize a benefit for us.

I also want to dedicate this book to my mom, Sue Hodges, who is eighty-six years old and volunteered to type this book for me: A Mother's Love!

1

A Well-Timed Song of Hope

I've been told that there are those
Who will learn how to fly.
And I've been told that there are those
Who will never die.
And I've been told that there are stars
That will never lose their shine.
And that there is a Morning Star
who knows my mind.

So why should I worry?
Why should I fret?
'Cause I've got a Mansion Builder
Who ain't through with me yet.

And I've been told that there's a
Crystal lake in the sky.
And every tear from my eyes
Is saved when I cry.
And I've been told there'll come a time
When the sun will cease to shine.
And that there is a Morning Star who knows my mind.

So why should I worry?
Why should I fret?
'Cause I've got a Mansion Builder
Who ain't through with me yet.
—"Mansion Builder" by 2nd Chapter of Acts, 1978

My story begins in the Temple ICU waiting room, where my family had gathered after I had suffered a heart attack and been air lifted to Temple. About five members of a family whose son had been severely hurt in a car accident came in and began playing their guitars and sang this beautiful song, which was such a great help to my family.

This book is my account of the last three years and my incredible journey with God, which has been super tough for me and my family and at the same time the most rewarding experience that a person could hope to have. This book is also an account of my life with Christ beginning in 1992, when my family was hit by a train and I promised God that I would be His servant for life if He would let everyone be okay.

He did, and I am His for life!

2

My Earlier Life

B ack in 1980 I was going through a divorce and I went on a yearlong binge of drinking, fighting, and running the bars every night. The saddest part of this was that my daughter, Melissa, wasn't even a year old at that time. Oh sure, I paid my child support and got her every other weekend, but I would just pick her up and take her straight to my mom's house and drop her off Friday, and not come back again until Sunday for lunch. I would play with her for a couple of hours before taking her home—some Dad, huh.

There were several times that year that I thought for sure I was going to be shot, but I just didn't care. On Halloween night I was at a bar and this pretty young woman came in and I went over and asked her to dance. She politely turned me down, not once, not twice, but three times. I finally asked her friend why she wouldn't dance with me and she said because of my bad reputation. After seeing her there several other times, she finally said yes and we danced. We both really felt perfect as dance partners.

She was going through a rough divorce also. Sometimes we would stay at a coffee shop talking and listening to the jukebox until 3:00 or 4:00 in the morning. I would never ask her out, because I knew I was the last thing she needed in her life right then. My birthday was coming up on New Year's Eve, and I asked her to go dancing with me. After that, we knew we had found true love. It took another three years for her to settle me down.

Most importantly, she taught me how to be a Dad again for my daughter, Melissa, and her daughter, Lindy, who was a year older than Melissa. Those two girls became close immediately.

On March 11, 1984, we were married and bought a house and fourteen acres of land near Somerville, Texas. It was an old farmhouse that required a lot of overhaul work to make it a home. We did a lot of land clearing and burning brush. It was hard work, but we did it together and we loved sitting by the fire and telling stories. On April 7, 1985 the Lord blessed us with twin boys, Jacob and John. Weighing just 4.1 pounds and 4.3 pounds, they were so small I could cup my hands and carry them around. Next came about six months of feeding the boys every two hours day and night. My wife and I would take turns all through the night. During these months, we were both like walking Zombies.

When the boys were about eighteen-months old, we noticed they were far behind other kids their age. Our doctor sent us to Texas Children's Hospital in Houston where they were tested by some doctors from Berkley, California. After doing some genetic tests, the twins were diagnosed with a disability called Williams Syndrome. While the doctors were doing some more testing, my wife and I visited the third floor where children suffering with cancer were being treated. I'll tell you one thing, when think you've got it bad, just take a look around and what you have doesn't seem as bad. All the years that followed have been so much fun: fishing, vacations, and reunions with my huge family. These boys who were sent to us from heaven have been such a joy to everyone they have met.

3

The Train Wreck

N ow, before 1992, I wasn't much of a Christian. I was what
I called a Christian of convenience. Oh, for sure I went to
church every Easter, Christmas, and a few other Sundays when
my wife kept nagging me about going. But all of this would all
change one early spring day in 1992.

I was in my office doing paperwork when the phone rang. I
picked it up and a lady yelled: "Steve, you've got to get to the train
tracks fast; your family has been hit by a train." Out the door I
ran, grabbing the first truck I came to. At that time, I had three
Dodge Cummins diesel trucks: one was five-speed and the other
two were automatics. The five-speed was closest, so I jumped
in and off to town I went as fast as I could go. It was then that I
realized that I had taken the one truck with a governor on it. It
would only let me go 85 mph!

As I turned the corner to the tracks, all I could see was police
cars, a firetruck, an ambulance, and a sea of people. Making my
way through the crowd, I could see our Chevy Astro van smashed
and upside down. Then I saw my daughter, Lindy, holding Jacob
and I saw the EMTs working on John on the ground. But I did not
see was my wife. I immediately ran to the van, and began yanking
on the van door and screaming her name. Several people had
to come and show me that she was down by John, and I just
didn't see her.

After loading John up, June and Jacob rode with him in the ambulance. Several people offered to drive me in to the hospital, but I thought I could keep up better myself. That was a bad choice as it turned out. Once the ambulance was underway, they left me behind in no time. I kept thinking; this must be really bad since they took off so fast. I was pleading and crying, begging God to let John be okay, and I promised Him I was His for life if He would just spare John. I was crying so bad that I left the road several times and I know for a fact that if I had taken one of those automatic trucks without the speed governor that would run 105–110 mph, we never would never have made it to the hospital. As it turned out, John had some swelling of his brain from the impact, but he recovered without any problem.

True to my word, I was now God's faithful servant for life!

4

The Shop

Before 1990, I had an oil field service company. I left for work at 5:00 or 5:30 each morning, and I didn't get home usually before 6:00 in the evening. Since we lived out of town, I never really got to meet very many people. I wanted to get into a business that wasn't dependent on the oil field industry because when oil crashes in Texas, so do all the service companies. In the '80s there had been two such times and many people were out of work.

I decided to change my business to an oil, lube, and tire business. Right away I started meeting and making friends with many area people. Over the next twenty-eight years, I made thousands of local friends. I shared their grief when a loved one died, and I always tried to personally wash their car at no charge before the funeral. I talked to so many of my customers who had cancer, heart disease, and other illnesses. One particular lady had been a customer from the week we opened and she came in one Saturday with a lawnmower flat. While she waited for my guys to fix it, we sat on the tailgate of her truck and talked. That's when she told me she had received bad news from her doctor. The doctor had told her that her cancer was back and there was nothing they could do. *Wow!* I sat there quiet for a few minutes, then jumped up and asked her if she had ever been to the Rocky Mountains. She said "No, why?" I told her that when I lived in West Texas, every weekend that I could I'd drive up into the mountains near

Ruidoso, New Mexico, and how close I would feel to God when I saw all the beauty and quietness. About three weeks later, she called and said, "Steve I took your advice. I drive every day to Lincoln National Forest, and yes, I do feel closer to God. I can't thank you enough." I think she lived another three months.

Being a local businessman, I also played mediator in some family quarrels. One spouse would come in and tell me about their spouse, and then the other would come in and tell me their side of the story. I would always do my best to bring them together. I would tell them about walking up on the Lake Somerville Dam where I ran every chance I got at daylight. There is a part of the dam that is blocked off for two miles. Many times, I would be finishing my 4-mile run and someone would just be getting there, and want to talk. I would walk another two or three miles just visiting and listening to their problems.

There was one particular guy who really bothered me. He was one of the most hateful, foul-mouthed people I had ever met. He had the worst outlook on life. Several times I had to ask him to leave if he couldn't clean up his mouth. The first time he left, but he came back the next week with a better attitude. This man had been in a bad big truck accident in Houston and got a big settlement. He had it made: all the money he needed, a nice brick home, nice truck, big ski boat, and fishing boat, and anything else he wanted. The one thing he didn't have was any love of himself or love of God. Several years later he came down with diabetes and soon lost both of his legs. This made him even madder at the world, but he always did better when he came to my shop. A few months after he'd lost his legs, he came in for an oil change and had to have a driver. When they stopped, he told me to get in. I noticed that his skin was very yellow. He said, "Steve, I am dying and I'm scared. I know you are a man of God and I need to talk to a priest." I gave him the number of a priest I knew. A few months later his brother came in and said he had died. I asked his brother if he had been able to talk to a priest. He said he didn't think so. I have so often wondered if there was more that I should have done.

To say the least, my twenty-eight years of having the shop were all so awesome. It was hard work, and full of problems, but I enjoyed it. With all the friends I made I can honestly say that I only had problems with maybe no more than forty people. This is a number I am proud of. In today's times, when people are just waiting for someone to make a mistake so they can jump all over them, how could I ever be so lucky to have dealt with thousands of people and only had forty that I refused to do business with. One man got so upset that I didn't call him to tell him his lawn mower tire had come in, even though I had called his wife and told her. He was in my office really giving it to me. I politely told him this was nothing to get so mad over. I told him: "Do you see my sons and how happy they are? I coach Special Olympics and these kids have all the reason to be bitter, but they are some of the happiest people I know." After telling him this, he got real quiet. I really feel sorry for people who go through life with such a chip on their shoulder.

That brings me to another specialty my shop offered. Every customer who came in was greeted by not one but two PR guys. Jacob and John were in charge of talking to the customers, and boy did they like doing that. When the person left, both of the boys knew the customer's name and what kind of weed eater, chainsaw, or mower they had. If the customer is was a rancher, they knew what kind of cows they had. If the customer was an oil field worker, they knew what kind of rig they were on or what kind of motor they had on their oil wells. If the customer was a railroad person, they knew all about their train or what they did. People will tell you fifteen or twenty years later that they still remember all these things, especially if the customer had a Harley Davidson motorcycle! Some of my friends would come by and take the boys for a ride on their bikes. I have had so many people tell me that when they came in to my shop, they were having a bad day, but when they left it was a much better day. Who could ask for better team of PR guys than this?

I loved doing business for Somerville. I loved being able to make so many friends. A man could not have been so lucky. Did I ever get "Rich"? No, but my reward was far from monetary. It was what I took home each and every day when I left the shop.

5

The Help

O ver twenty-eight years in business, I had the opportunity
to work with twelve to fifteen hundred employees. I gave
many young men their first job. They learned the way I learned
from my dad: Number one, you learned what hard work was;
Number two, you learned to do it right the first time or you did it
over; and Number three, you learned how to respect *all* the customers, which is something you almost never find anymore; and
lastly, you learned what being on time to work meant.

I was taught it was better to be to work fifteen to thirty minutes early than to be late. On Saturday we opened at 7:00 instead
of 8:00, so we could give our shop a real cleanup. These young
men always seemed to go out on Friday nights and just couldn't
get to work on time Saturday morning. I really didn't mind fifteen or twenty minutes, but after that I had a really good remedy.
We always had 100–150 old tires stacked up in back of the shop.
When those Friday night revelers would come dragging in late,
I'd tell them to go out back and move that whole stack of tires
over about twenty or thirty feet. Now, I don't know if you've ever
moved old tires, but they were usually filled with water and they
had steel belts showing. Also, in Texas, the humidity can be terrible, especially if you had been out partying the night before.
Believe me, it didn't take more than two times of doing this and
these boys learned to be on time. Today they'd probably put me
in jail for this. It was always so neat to watch these young men

go on to be successful in life. You wouldn't believe how many would come back and tell me thanks for teaching them how to work and how to respect the customer. They could see how this had helped them in their work and lives.

I also gave jobs to several kids who were already in trouble. Some were on drugs or had already gotten in trouble with the law—just minor stuff. I would talk and mentor these young men, and I saw several who were able to turn their lives around. Some of them turned out to be the best hands I had. One of the best hands I ever had, and I considered him more like a son, was a young man who was working at Dairy Queen when I hired him. We called him "DeBo." This young man later became my shop manager for more than five years while he was going to school to become a preacher. I think he is now in West Virginia working over at the Fellowship of Christian Athletes Organization.

Another young man named Rodney worked for me part-time for more than fourteen years. He also worked in the oilfield four days on and three days off. This young man really knew how to work and was also one of my good friends. We both liked to dove hunt and go crappie and white bass fishing at Lake Somerville. He was a great family man with three sons. And he loved being a little league baseball coach. Unfortunately, he was killed in a tractor accident. This was one of those moments when you ask yourself, "Why did it have to happen to such a great person like this," but we don't know God's reason.

6

The Hand of God

Back in 1983 when I bought the shop, it had an upstairs, and had a perfect place to put up a basketball hoop. One of my very first employees and I put a backboard up that we had found in the landfill dump. It was just starting to burn. We later learned that this was from the old gym in Snook, a town about fifteen miles away. This was the beginning of thirty-eight years of thousands of games of Horse, 2 on 2, and Around the World. I would joke when hiring a new hand that one of the job requirements was that you had to play basketball. You should have seen the look on some of the older men that I hired!

On April 6, 2000, we were finishing out the day with a game of 3 on 3. My shop had two sixteen-foot doors on it, one facing east and the other facing south. My friend, Rodney, was playing back under the goal while, me, my nephew, Brian and three other employees were right in the front door. Suddenly, Rodney yelled "Look out!" My shop was located at a very busy intersection and we had seen lots of wrecks. Normally everyone would have stopped and looked at the intersection, but this time with one sweep of His hand, we were all pushed away from the front door. Immediately, Brian and I were hit by something that crushed both of us to the floor. As we slid along the floor, we were face to face. When we stopped, I said, "Brian, what just happened?" All he could say was "I don't know, but it's bad." In just a matter of minutes, some men lifted the door off of us and dragged us

13

out of the building to the back. I kept asking what had happened, but nobody would tell me. The DPS later told me the truck hit us going about 75 mph and the driver never hit his brakes. We never even heard the crash.

After the ambulance arrived, I got back up and was able to hobble around to see what had happened. There, where Brian and I and the others had been standing, was an eighteen-wheeler truck. When I saw the shop door, I realized that only six inches were between where Brian and I were and the wheel of that truck. Man, I felt weak. That evening, even though I was hurting, I stayed until 10:00 pm working with about a dozen of my customers trying to get everything of value out of the shop. A friend of mine was a police officer in Somerville, and he said he would stay out there all night to make sure no one tried to steal anything.

When I got home all I could do was sit in my chair with my eyes wide open. Around 6:30 the next morning, I went back to the shop. As I was walking around when, all of a sudden, my legs started to buckle. My police friend helped me to the tailgate of my truck where I started throwing up severely. Afraid I was having a heart attack; he called for an ambulance and called my wife who was the secretary of the elementary school. By the time she got there, they were loading me up and had started an IV. Immediately I felt better and told my wife I didn't think I needed to go to the hospital. "No way," she told me. As it turned out, I'd had a small concussion, bruised ribs, a hematoma on my thigh, and my ankle was really bruised. Every place that the ribs on the door hit me was bruised.

People kept asking me, how much I was going to sue the trucking company for. I told them all I didn't believe in doing that and that was what was wrong with America. How can someone sue McDonalds over spilling hot coffee on yourself while driving. Everyone is just waiting for something to happen so they can sue. The trucking company insurance took care of everything and paid all my help while they were off work. My shop was rebuilt and once again we were able to play basketball.

Again, all I can say is we felt the Hand of God that day! He saved us and I am thankful.

7

Special Olympics

After attending a junior college and running track, I went to work as a bricklayer, which is what I had done for a couple of years during the summer for our neighbor. My boss started up a slow-pitch softball team and I played center field. Then I got on a traveling team and went to tournaments all around the area. After that I played some from 1976–2000 until after the shop wreck. My daughter, Lindy, was my team bookkeeper for many years. In fact, that was where she met her husband, Chris, who played third base for me. From the time my twin boys were in a stroller, they had been going to games and tournaments. After the shop wreck, my leg was never the same, so I retired from softball; that's when June and I decided to start a Special Olympics team in Somerville since they didn't have one there. We were joined in coaching by Kim Z., Charles W., and Anita C., who drove our bus.

I remembered when the boys were in elementary school and they announced about little league baseball, the boys came home talking about getting on a team. Well, now was their chance to be on a team. I think that first couple of years we had about fourteen kids on our team. I'll never forget the first track meet we went to. One of our kids, Josh was in the 25-meter walk and he won first place and got a gold medal. I think he wore it to school every day for a week. We learned what it took to make each of the kids want to compete. For one girl, Stacy, it was me standing at the finish line with a teddy bear. Only one problem with that was when we went to the regional track meet, they wouldn't let me stand on the track, so when they fired the gun for the 50-meter walk, she got close to the finish line and came straight to me instead of the finish line. Of course, that was a joy to my wife and me.

One athlete named Jason was in a wheelchair, and at practice I'd race him while hopping on one foot or jumping backwards. You know what? I never did beat him.

One year we took Jacob and John to the state track meet in San Marcus, Texas. This was awesome as they were chosen to carry the torch with thousands of law enforcement officers escorting them in with sirens blaring. Talk about Goosebumps, we had them. Jacob competed in the 100-meter dash, which he won first place out of 283 runners with a time of 11.3 from a standup start and softball throw; while John was in the 50-meter dash and soft-ball throw. In the softball throw they got first and second with a throw just three feet apart. Now, is that twins or what?

The next week, we got a call from a lady who helped coach the National Track team and wanted to know if Jacob would like to be part of her team. He would have to go to Colorado that summer for one week. When we asked him, his reply was simply "No, not if Dad isn't my coach." You see, prestige and being first was no big deal to him. He didn't even realize how good he was but that didn't matter. Later that year, a lady from Conroe, Texas, called and wanted to know if the boys and I would like to play on a unified softball team. Unified is where half the team is special and the other half are regular players. Although they had never played baseball before, we did it. How awesome for me to get to play softball with my sons. After getting them each new gloves, we started playing catch three feet apart, then at six, ten, and fifteen feet. The next three years, we won state two out of three years and got invited to National again. We had four players who were in their forties and they simply said "no." I thought they were afraid of flying and offered to take them in my car, but again they said "no." So we had to withdraw after that.

The joys and rewards June and I got from our nine years of coaching Special Olympics and being chosen as Special Olympic Family of the Year cannot be touched with any amount of money.

A short time after this, Josh got sick and passed away. At his funeral we all sat on the front row with our Special Olympic shirts on. After this Jacob and John said they were through playing ball and dropped out of competing. They remained good friends with Josh's dad until he passed away and joined Josh in heaven.

8

Spring, 2018

S pringtime, my favorite time of the year! The crappie start running up the creeks to spawn in late February–March. Our family has been fishing the creeks for over forty-five years. The memories we have made are unreal. Even when my boys were in car seats, they would go with me. One year I bought a large wagon just for the purpose of pulling them up to the creek to fish with me. Then in April and May, the white bass start schooling. It was nothing for me to catch sixty or seventy fish—with eighteen to twenty keepers—every time I went fishing after work.

My favorite time to go fishing was Sunday morning. I would go for my 4-mile run and then wade out about waist deep and start catching fish. One Sunday I had waded out and had caught a fish when I had a pain in my chest just as I caught it. I thought it must just be gas or something. It went away pretty fast and I kept fishing. About twenty minutes later, I got another slightly stronger pain that went away pretty quickly, so I kept fishing. Finally, there was a much stronger pain, and I knew it wasn't gas. This one made me double over. The first thing I had to do was get out of the water. When I got to the shore, I was wondering if I should call 911, and as I just stood there wondering for about ten minutes, it went away. I loaded up and got to the house, but didn't tell June because I knew she would insist that I get it checked out. After that everything seemed to be normal. In June of that year around 3:00 am I had a dream and Jesus appeared and said

"Steve, it's time to let go." I woke up the next morning wondering what He meant for me to let go of. I just really didn't understand what He was saying or what He wanted me to do. I went on to work. Nothing had changed except I knew deep down what Jesus meant by "letting go." You see, since 2011 when I lost my good friend, Rodney, I never really had anyone who I could rely on as a shop manager. This left it all up me to do the invoices, sales, and I had no time off.

My wife and daughters had been telling me for years to sell my shop so I could start enjoying our family more. I was not able to take off to go on vacations with them to the beaches in Alabama, Port Aransas, or any place for that matter. My only vacation was a three-day weekend on holidays. They could all tell the stress was starting to get to me. I was constantly having to train new hands because I was firing so many for not showing up to work for days at a time or for showing up multiple times with alcohol on their breath or smelling like marijuana. Then there were all the mistakes that are bound to happen with new help such as forgetting to tighten drain plugs, breaking the tire sensor, for taking pin stripes off cars with our pressure cleaner, etc., etc. And I was having to pay for all of these mistakes.

Gone were the days when all of us were playing basketball, playing dominoes, or cards. Now, it was every time we were slow, they would all go to their car or truck to smoke a cigarette because I wouldn't allow smoking the shop. I blame a lot of these mistakes on cell phones. You don't know how many times I would walk up and catch them on their cell phones while changing someone's oil or tire. More than once I had to break up a near fight and I'm talking grown men in their 40s. Anyhow, you get the picture, the stress of running the shop without a manager was getting to me. So, yes, I did know what Jesus was talking about letting go of.

9

The Day

On August 7, the boys and I came home from the shop and I told my wife it was so hot that instead of going for my 4-mile run, I was going to do my swimming workout. She said she would come get me when supper was almost ready, as she always did.

At that time, I had three workouts that I did: one was running four miles in our twenty-four-foot above ground pool, which was 212 laps. Another was holding on to the ladder and doing about 5,000 bicycle crunches. The last was one-half mile of under-water swimming, which was 44 laps. Away I went. When I got to lap 22, all of a sudden it felt like my chest was caving in. I remember pulling myself up to the side of the pool and seeing my wife standing right there. I told her it was my heart. That was the last thing I said or saw for the next seven or eight weeks.

As I slipped under the water, my wife jumped in and pulled me up. I was completely blue. I immediately started throwing up water and then more water. Now, on most days my boys went to their rooms and put on their headphones to listen to music and rest when we came home. On this day, Jacob didn't have his on and heard June calling him. When he came out and saw her in the pool, he thought that I had thrown her in and we were playing. But he saw it was serious and ran to get the phone for June. She called 911. We live in a remote area and only have one ambulance. If it is out on a call, the closest ambulance is in Caldwell, which is about twenty miles away. This day, they were in Somerville and got there in about fifteen minutes. After getting me out of the water, they immediately started CPR, but realizing how serious this was they called for a Life Flight. Two of my brothers live in the county and one heard the call and immediately came to our house. They got to see the paramedics shocking me.

When the helicopter got there, they had to land on the Davidson Creek bridge right below our house. As soon as they got me loaded into the helicopter, we headed for St. Joseph's Hospital in Bryan, Texas, about thirty miles north. The doctors there told my wife that I needed to be in surgery within an hour. They also called Msg. John Malinoski in and he gave me my Last Rites with my wife and daughters there. Then, they let my mom and brothers in to say goodbye. After loading me back into the helicopter, we headed for Baylor Scott & White-Temple Hospital where a heart surgeon, Dr. Lee, was waiting. Once there it was determined that I'd had an Aortic Cardiac Aneurysm dissection, which is the worst kind of heart attack. Dr. Lee told my family that this kind of heart attack was very serious, and the prospect of being successful wasn't very good because it had been so long in getting me there. The one thing I had on my side was the fact that I was in such good shape. He told them he would do everything he could to be successful. I then underwent a ten-and-one-half hour surgery, during which I suffered two mini-strokes.

10

A Ray of Hope in the Night

T hat night, my family was gathered in the waiting room while I was in surgery. All of a sudden, the door to the waiting room opened very quietly—they were usually very loud when opening—in walked a beautiful older lady with shoulder-length white hair. She was dressed all in white. She walked straight over to my son-in-law Chris and took his hand and talked to him. After a few minutes she walked right into the ICU and a few minutes later the doors to the ICU opened and a bright light flooded the waiting room. The lady stepped into the door with her white cape. Everyone thought to themselves, *She looks just like an angel,* but no one said anything because, as tired as they all were they thought maybe they were imagining this. The lady then walked back to my son-in-law Chris and took his hand and spoke: "I was here for an old friend who was dying and had no family and was scared to die alone. But know this, the one you are here for is going to be all right. You will not see me again." She then turned and walked to the elevator and was gone. It wasn't until the next morning when someone said, "You will never believe what I saw or dreamed last night!" Then everyone shared that they too had seen this.

This was also the time when the family whose son has been in the wreck came in and sang the beautiful song I've placed at the beginning of this book. I have it on my phone and listen to it often. They harmonized it to perfection and this was a big gift for my family.

After the completion of my surgery, Dr. Lee came out and explained that he had repaired my heart and now we would have to wait and see how I did. He gave me about a forty to fifty percent chance of making it. During the surgery I had suffered two mini strokes, so I have had complications to deal with from that also. I didn't wake up for several weeks after the surgery.

11

"You Will Soon Witness a Miracle"

After a couple of weeks in ICU in Temple, they told us that it was time to find a long-term ICU hospital. My daughters, Lindy and Melissa, began the search, driving all over the place visiting different hospitals. Two of those they visited actually made them cry because they knew from the looks how depressing they were. They finally found Kindred Hospital in Tomball, Texas. This one looked more like what they were hoping to find.

June's sister and her husband brought their travel trailer to Tomball and parked it in a park just about two miles from the hospital for them to stay in. As June was packing up from the hotel, she saw some Chinese Fortune cookies from the night before and put them in her purse. Later that day, she opened one to eat it and the fortune inside said "You will soon witness a miracle!" This was a couple of weeks before I woke up. We still have this fortune cookie strip taped to our bathroom mirror in our home.

12

Waking Up

W hat a way to wake up. The very first thing I remember was opening my eyes and seeing someone sitting on my chest trying to stick something down my nose and hollering, "Swallow, Swallow!" You can't imagine how scared I was. I couldn't speak because of the trach tube I had, and I was strapped down and couldn't move my arms. My wife and Melissa were there and said I went totally nuts. I was fighting, my eyes were bulged out, and I finally broke my right arm free and knocked whoever this was sitting on me off of my chest. My wife told the nurse, "I don't know what you gave him, but this is not my husband." She later told me that I looked like a trapped animal fighting for its life. Wow: What a way to wake up.

They finally asked my wife and daughter to help hold me down and still were unsuccessful placing the tube. My wife finally told them to stop and get someone in there who knew what they were doing. A respiratory nurse named Tammy came in to help and came over to me and started rubbing my head and almost immediately, I calmed down. The doctor said not to try anymore until the next day.

Thank goodness, the next day I was able to swallow and didn't have to have a feeding tube inserted. This meant I could have soft foods; I think they called it puréed. I'll be the first to tell you I prefer meat and potatoes, but this was so much better than a feeding tube.

The hardest thing for me at this point was not being able to talk. After a whole life of talking, I couldn't make a sound. One time one of my brothers and his wife came to visit. I kept pointing at him then pointing to myself, then circling my finger and pointing outside. I did this over and over. My wife went and bought a little chalk board and I wrote "You, me, Go!" He said he cried all the way home that day.

13

My Life at Kindred Hospital

W hen I was able to start looking at my body, I think that at one time I had five tubes or hoses coming out of me. There were wires hooked up all over the place as well as to two IV stands. I remember thinking, *What in the world has happened to me?* After about a week, I was able to understand what had happened. I couldn't remember a thing, but June and I started talking about it.

We realized what a hand God had played in all of this. If June had come out five minutes earlier, I would have said I will get a few more laps in before I quit. If she had come out a few minutes later, the results could have been worse.

The next several weeks were a blur of hallucinations and dreams that were mostly terrible, though some were awesome. I think the worst one was one when my brother Eddie, and I were in a parking lot and I was carrying a jar of spiderlings (little spiders). I dropped it and those little spiders went everywhere. Eddie and I were terrified.

In another dream, I was in Galveston on a dock with a bunch of Korean doctors all around me. There was a huge black ship out in the bay and it had gold lights all over it. After they loaded me on the ship we took off into the sky where they were operating on me. Some kind of crazy dream.

One really great dream was when God gave me a slideshow of my life. It started when I was in high school running track. Next,

I saw my ex-wife and me in the mountains and then I saw my baby daughter. Next, I saw June when we first met. The neatest one was of my twin boys when they were just born. They were so tiny and I was holding both of them. Then I saw so many pictures of my shop. It all brought back so many memories. It was an awesome dream.

I remember when one of nurses came in, it looked like she had a bandolier full of meds. It would take them probably ten minutes to shoot all those into my IV. They were eventually able to get my pneumonia under control, and several weeks later they were finally able to remove my trach tube so once again I could talk.

Several mornings, I could see my work shirt and jeans on the dresser. I could also see my Toyota truck in the parking lot outside my room. I would try and try to get over to my clothes so I could go to the coffee shop and meet my friend and coffee drinking partner, Jimmy. For over thirty years we had met each morning and we'd had coffee together. But I couldn't move anything on my left side. I couldn't understand what was going on. It was crazy but I could smell coffee each morning about 5:30 and I'd ask the nurses if I could have a cup, but they would tell me they didn't have any coffee yet; I would have to wait until the cafeteria opened. When my wife got there each morning, I would ask her to get me some of that coffee I smelled and she would ask them and they would tell her they didn't have any. She just started bringing me a cup each morning. Another strange thing had happened, and I didn't find this out until last year when I called my old coffee drinking buddy, Jimmy, to see how he was doing. On the morning after my heart attack, he had been taken to the hospital for his diabetes and didn't go for coffee either. So, neither of us had shown up. We would always call each other to tell if we weren't going to be there, but we'd both missed our last morning.

In the first picture taken of me in the hospital at Tomball, I was sitting in a wheel chair. At this time, I wasn't even awake yet, but my physical therapist, Jessica, got me up and put my cap on. Talk about a crazy picture. Here I was with a trach tube, my hat on crooked, my eyes closed and in a hospital gown and not moving at all. This physical therapist was a real nut, but I really liked her. She was good and knew just how to handle me. One day as she got me up trying to stand, I made the mistake of telling her I couldn't feel my left leg. She reached down and pinched my calf really hard and said, "Do you feel that?" I never made that mistake again. It turned out I was paralyzed on my entire left side: my sight, my hearing, all the way down. Even my brain was paralyzed. The next few weeks were full of firsts: My first steps, my first little puzzle, my first simple math paper, my first picking up colored pegs and putting them on a board matching the colors. I have videos of most of these showing how Jessica and Jared got me to take my first steps, and then eventually be able to walk to the gym where I'd work on my left hand. Slowly, with their help and encouragement, my mind and left side were starting to work again. The one thing I wasn't able to master at Tomball was being able to read the clock on the wall. I'd tell my wife what time it was and she'd correct me over and over.

I remember the first time I got to go outside, and how the warm air hit me and how great it felt. One of my favorite treats was when June would bring me a chocolate shake. Nothing has ever tasted so good. One Saturday my brothers Eddie and Larry and their wives Tammy and Theresa and my nieces Madison and Whitney all came to visit. Most of the time if I was in bed, I would just doze off. This day while I was sleeping, I opened my eyes to see Eddie and Larry each massaging my feet as they said this would help get the circulation and nerves working. I always said I wish I had a picture of this. Then Larry shaved me and Theresa gave me a shampoo and a haircut. Madison and Whitney gave me a manicure and pedicure. Talk about feeling like a king. The nurse kept stopping and watching all this. Now this is family.

I can honestly say my stay at Kindred was great and I owe so much to all the doctors, nurses and therapists, and to all of my family and friends who came to visit me and encourage me to keep working hard. I would like to especially thank my physical therapists, Jessica and Jared, and my occupational therapist, Janice. It is really amazing how awesome they are at their jobs!

14

The Dream

One day my brother Eddie came to visit me at the hospital and I was telling him what all we could sell, and how much to sell it for, etc. That night, after he left, my mind was going in a hundred different directions. I was wondering what was going to happen to my family; how were we going to pay for all these doctor bills; what would happen to the business? I just couldn't get all of this out of my mind. Somewhere around 10:00 pm, I started praying the Our Father prayer over and over to try to push all this from my mind. At some point, I fell asleep. Later that night I had a dream.

The dream started with Eddie and me walking around the shop and Eddie was writing down everything I could sell. When we finished, he pulled his truck and gooseneck trailer across the highway from the shop. We were standing at the back of the trailer when a late '60s model teal green sports car with big racing slicks and black racing stripes pulled up beside us. I halfway looked over and nodded, then I turned back to Eddie. When he didn't leave, I looked back and I saw Jesus Christ at the wheel of the sports car, and He looked straight into my eyes. His gaze seemed to go straight to my soul. He simply said, "Steve, don't worry, I've got this" and He held out the palm of His hand to me. Who could be so lucky to have this happen to them? I then woke up crying, and asked Lindy—who was staying with me that night at the hospital—to put the Rosary on and we prayed. I completely calmed down after that and fell back to sleep.

Later, Deacon John from St. Mary's Church in Caldwell came to visit me and brought me a beautiful little quilt with a prayer for healing on it. It was made by some ladies from the church. I carried this blanket everywhere I went, even if it was just for an MRI. It brought me so much comfort and I have several pictures of me in bed or in my wheel chair with this blanket.

15

Moving on to St. Joseph Rehab

Sometime around September 15, it came time for me to move from the ICU hospital to a long-term rehab facility. Once again, my daughters started going from place to place to find a rehab that was covered by our insurance. And once again what they found was worse than the ICUs. Luckily, we knew someone who worked at St. Joseph's Hospital in Bryan, which was only thirty minutes from home. She was able to connect us with someone who was able to get me approved through my insurance to go there. The only problem was there weren't any rooms available there. We were down to just one day until we had to make a decision.

On September 23, a room in the facility in Bryan became open. Once again this was a blessing from above. It meant that my family and a lot of my friends from Somerville could now come and visit. When they came, I enjoyed their visits so much, but I think I talked their ears off. Most importantly, my boys could come and visit whenever they wanted to.

I've got a great story: I arrived at St. Joe's Rehab on a Friday night and thirty or forty of my family members were there to greet me. On the ride from Tomball when the ambulance passed Texas Speedway and I saw the College Station city limits sign, I started crying.

By the time we got to the rehab hospital, I was so exhausted. I think I slept most of that weekend. On Monday morning I was asleep when I felt someone shaking me and telling me to wake up. When I opened my eyes there was a lady dressed all in white with a white head covering. You will never know what I thought: *Is this?* or *Am I?* But thankfully, it was just my therapist named Allia. I soon found out that she is one of the very best at working with stroke victims.

That first morning, our goal was learning how to transfer from the bed to the wheelchair. We did this over and over until I got it right. Then the occupational therapist came and I had to put my shoes and socks on and try to tie my shoelaces. This didn't happen for several days. Next, the therapist who worked with my mind came. She gave me more and more puzzles to work and more math problems. It didn't take but a couple of days and I was able to complete them and even tell time again.

A few mornings later I still could barely move my left leg. I had been trying and trying but I just couldn't make it move. I dropped the TV remote and just rolled over with my left leg. I was so happy I called June at 4:00 in the morning. Soon after this, Allia wheeled me down to the gym and stopped by some stairs. She told me to stand up and go up five steps. I told her there was no way I could do this. You know I should have learned this in Tomball, but you can never say, "I can't do this" or "I can't do that" when you're working with a therapist. Believe it or not, I was able to stand up and go up those steps. I was so scared and I was shaking all over, but I made it. The next few weeks were amazing. Finally the time came for me to walk by myself. Allia told me to stand up and walk about thirty feet. I started to say I don't think I can do that, but instead I stood up and I did it. It was just amazing how they know just how to work with their patients.

Another great experience I had while I was at St. Joseph Rehab; I met a World War II veteran who was 105 years old. He had flown the orders over to General McArthur to deploy the

Atomic Bomb. What an amazing man he was. We had several good visits while we were there, and I think he just died last year.

One Sunday when I was getting stronger, my wife and I went to church at the chapel. Msg. John Malinoski did the Mass. He was the same one who had read me my Last Rites on the day of my heart attack. After Mass he told me, "I never expected to see you alive again."

Another awesome moment that I experienced while I was there was one Sunday morning when I started feeling prayers coming into my mind. They just flooded in. It felt like they were coming from a church across the street—Mt. Zion Missionary Church with Rev. Basil Lister as pastor. I knew so many of that congregation. This really cheered me up.

Then, just thirteen days after arriving, I walked down the hall about fifty feet all by myself. I turned around and walked back to my wheelchair, backed up and sat down. I felt like I had flown to the moon. It was such a big accomplishment. Allia eventually let me walk outside with her right behind me just in case I should get unsteady, she could grab the gate belt to steady me. I was now doing much harder puzzles and math problems. My mind was finally waking up.

Then, on October 10, I was scheduled to be released. What a wonderful feeling when I walked out of those front doors and got into our SUV to head home.

16

Home Life

When I got home, the emotional impacts of where I had come from and where I was now hit me full force. There was just so much I couldn't do anymore. I was really weak. When I had my heart attack, I weighed 188 pounds; when I left St Joseph's rehab, I was down to 142 pounds. Most of the loss was muscle mass.

My brother-in law, Eddie, built a nice ramp off the back of our house, which made it so much easier for me. I was still getting used to my walker and several times I would catch the walker on the rug and fall. I think I fell about six times in all. One time I landed right on my tail bone and really bruised it good.

It was nice to be in my own bed after being in a hospital bed for two and a half months. The doctors decided I was ready to start outpatient rehab. This was done at St. Joseph's as well. I had two days a week of rehab, which meant June had to take me to Bryan, wait for me to do the rehab and drive us back home. She certainly had her hands full; not only taking care of my needs, but doing all the mowing, taking care of our goats as well as her usual cooking, cleaning, laundry, and seeing to the twins' needs. She was a real trooper and never complained. This was her home and family and she enjoyed it.

Our home was on Davidson Creek, and there were all kinds of wildlife nearby: deer, hogs, and snakes, especially copper heads, all loved the sandy soil. She and the boys got really good at scaring the hogs away from our yard. She would come across a whole lot of snakes while doing work outside in our garden or tending to our three rows of Brazos Berries. The berries really took a lot of work especially around May when they started ripening. She would pick twelve to fifteen gallons of berries each year. Back when we were coaching Special Olympics, I had five huge rows of berries and I would usually get around forty to fifty gallons a year. After putting up ten to twelve gallons for us, I'd take the rest up to the shop and sell them, with the money I made going to our Special Olympics team. This allowed us to have some really neat shirts and now and then buy a kid some tennis shoes to run in. It also gave us money to stop and eat sometimes.

June really had to take over doing all her work plus everything I used to do. This made me feel useless, and a bit depressed. But, I was making progress at rehab and getting stronger. I liked doing small step-ups and step-downs and learning how to walk sideways and backwards. Soon I was stepping over cones both sideways and front and I could feel myself improving. Then, on a Sunday morning, November 11, I woke up feeling really bad. I could tell my blood pressure was high, so June checked it and sure enough it was 180/96. This was a terrible feeling, so June called an ambulance and off we went to the hospital. I stayed in the hospital for days while they ran all kinds of tests. My heart doctor wanted to make sure I hadn't had another stroke. Unfortunately, it turned out that I did have one and about the only thing that it had affected was my left foot, which had cupped and turned inward. This doctor wanted me to go back and see Dr. Lee, the doctor who had done my surgery, because he was afraid something from my heart may have caused this. I couldn't get an appointment with Dr. Lee until January, so once again we were on pins and needles waiting. I got to go home from the hospital on November 15 still not knowing for sure what had caused that stroke.

17

The Benefit

Everyone who knew me knew how much I loved to run, so my son-in-law, Kiley, thought of the perfect Bible verse to use, Hebrews 12:1 "and let us run with endurance the race that is set before us." And Steve's Race then became the name for the battle of my life. The kids had a big banner made and put it on the fence at my shop so that people could stop by and sign it or leave me a message.

It was also the theme of my Facebook page where everyone could keep up with my progress and also the theme of one of the largest benefits in Burleson County. My family, along with several friends, especially Travis, Chris, and Barbie planned a benefit for me. You would never believe the number of my family and members of our community who came together to help. They ordered special "Steve's Race" T-shirts and sold out of them. It was a one-day event that began with a 5K run, which was sponsored by several of the friends I had walked or run with over the years. There was also a turkey shoot where people brought their guns and tried to get the most pellets in the bullseye shooting at it blind from the backside. One company donated jump houses for the kids. There was a motorcycle run, a silent auction, and a live auction, which was huge. Also, there was a cake auction, and the biggest draw was a dance that night by a local band, Texas Unlimited Band, or TUB as it is known around here. My nephew

Cody Joe Hodges also drove in all the way from Nashville to perform that night!

They also had a huge BBQ plate dinner. All this was only possible because of my many friends and family members who did all the cooking and work; such a wide variety of people all working together to make it a success. In all there were about seventy or seventy-five people who volunteered and they sold over 1,200 plates! The benefit was so large that cars were lined up for eight city blocks waiting to get plates to go. At one point the police were threatening to shut it down because of the traffic, but Travis and my brother Eddie talked them out of it.

This event was started by Travis who just wanted to help us out. As you can imagine I was still very weak and knew I couldn't stay the whole day. I went to the first event, the 5K run, and rode in a Ranger with my brother Eddie to see and cheer my friends on while they ran. After this I was so tired, I had to go home and rest. At lunch I came back and could hardly walk around because of the big crowd. Then it was time for the auction to begin. My friend Buda was the auctioneer and did a great job. Because there were so many items, they had to have several sessions.

I wanted to try to thank everyone for all their support, but all I could do was sit and watch. You can't imagine how many people walked up to me and put a check in my hand. Talk about making a person deeply emotional. I had always been the type that thought men didn't cry, but that day, I couldn't control myself. Maybe it was the medicine, or how weak I was, but on this day, this man cried.

After lunch I was exhausted and had to go back home and rest until around 4:00 in the afternoon. By 7:00, it was still going strong. Mayor Waylon Edwards, who has been my friend for many years, called my family and I up to the front of the stage. That is when he gave a speech on my life and all I had done for our community. He then presented me with a plaque for the town's

Outstanding Citizen Award and declared this an annual award for someone nominated for the Steve Hodges Outstanding Citizen Award. He also presented me with a Proclamation Award from the county judge and three county commissioners. It said that November 17 each year would be designated as Steve Hodges Day in Burleson County. Could any man ever hope to be so lucky to have this many friends. Once again, I became emotional.

The benefit continued on into the evening and I went home totally worn out. This was by far the largest benefit that I had ever seen and I had gone to so many over the years to help people including some I didn't know.

After all was said and done, they had raised around $93,000. They will never know how much this helped us out. Right off the bat, we owed $48,000 for the two Life Flight rides and the bills just kept coming in. I asked my wife, "Don't we have insurance for that?" She said, yes but a lot of these things weren't covered. Without this benefit, we would have been in debt for a lot of money for a very long time. As it turned out, we were able to pay all our bills and had some left over for the next year's doctor bills.

All I can say is "God Bless these good people who worked so hard to make this benefit a success!"

18

2019

In January 2019, it was time for my 6 month follow up appointment with Dr. Lee, the heart surgeon in Temple. Once again, I went through the whole regimen of tests to see whether something with my heart had caused the stroke. That afternoon we met with Dr. Lee and the other surgeons who had helped with my surgery. When they came in, you could tell that Dr. Lee was excited to see that I had made it. He told us that when they first got the news that I was being flown from Bryan that night and knowing how long it had been since my heart attack, all the other doctors discussed how they doubted I would even make it to Temple from Bryan, much less survive any surgery. But Dr. Lee was determined and said "we just have to try to save him." And I am so thankful he did. After looking at all the tests, Dr. Lee determined that my heart did not cause the stroke and that I wouldn't need another surgery. Once again, as we left Temple that day, I cried.

Now it was time to decide what to do with my business. It was obvious to us that I wasn't physically or mentally going to be able to work anymore. We decided to start clearing out my shop and get ready to either sell or lease it out. Thank goodness in 2018 I had been able to pay off my truck and then two months before my heart attack, I had completely paid off my business debts. Again, God had a plan allowing me to be debt free before I got sick. This meant we were in no hurry to do anything.

My awesome sister-in-law and her husband, Connie and Randy, as well as my brothers, Eddie and Larry, went to work helping June start cleaning and getting my inventory returned. When you have twenty-eight years of paperwork and a shop that needed a really good cleaning, you don't realize until you start going through all of it what an ordeal it could be. My family worked tirelessly making hundreds of trips to the dump, cleaning the shop, and sorting through all my tools. It took several weeks to get things in order. It didn't take long to find someone to lease the shop and when they took over in February; that took a huge weight off our backs.

As I have mentioned before, we raised goats on our land. Well, the goats had really torn up some of our fences during this time and were constantly getting out, and June would have to go try to get them back in. That's when Randy and Connie came to our rescue again. They replaced the whole fence, which was around thirty years old. I don't know what we would have done without these two. Again, I sat in the house feeling so useless watching them all working and not being able to do anything to help.

19

Looking for that Miracle!

W hen I came home from the hospital, I kept waiting for that miracle in the fortune cookie. I prayed every day for God to let it happen. I just knew any day now it was going to happen. But, of course, only God knows how and when that is to be.

As days turned to months, I started to feel hopeless. As you will see, I found my miracle - two and a half years later.

20

Getting Stronger

Mid-January, I was released from outpatient rehab. We found a gym that was for fifty-five and older adults. It had some of the best equipment, so I joined. I saw pretty quickly that I needed help in learning how to use some of the weight machines. We were able to get a personal trainer. This lady was awesome and helped me so much. I went two times a week.

I had worked out all my life and I thought I knew what "No pain, no gain" meant, but I can tell you one thing, I had never hurt so much ever. I just couldn't believe I was so weak. I was doing great until April. We had gone to church in Caldwell Saturday night. Mass had just started when a sharp pain hit my back, then my left foot started clenching and turning in. I told June we had to go and go now. When we got in the car she wanted to know if she needed to call 911. I sat there a minute and said no, just start driving to the hospital, which was about forty miles from Caldwell. As we headed out, I started getting worse. June pulled over and got the blood pressure monitor out. She kept one at home and one in the car. When she read the pressure, we knew this was bad for it was 230/120. She dialed 911 and they picked me up on Highway 21. On the way to the hospital the EMTs had to give me sprays of nitro. In my mind, I knew it was another stroke and I was so scared.

Arriving at the hospital, it was a real emergency with doctors and nurses working on me. Again, the next five days were filled with test after test. The good news was that I had not had another stroke. It was determined that one of meds that the doctors had decreased was the cause of the spike in my blood pressure.

The next week I was able to return to the gym. I was steadily improving, so they added a half hour of working in the studio on balance and walking without the walker. I was even able to start walking at the track with a cane. You don't know how good it felt to be back at the track and to see some of the people who used to see me all the time running. I was really proud. One day June even took me to the Somerville dam to walk. I was on top of the world. I actually drove my truck to the house from my shop, which is fifteen miles away, and next I was able to get on our zero-turn mower. It was really hard to get on but I felt useful again, because I could do something to help. June even sent videos to my family of me mowing and walking. I can't believe how good it felt.

I had a vision of me getting up at daybreak and going to the dam by myself to walk with my cane. I just couldn't wait to be able to do that.

In April I started doing pool workouts. All of this was very challenging. It was really demanding on my muscles and body. After the third workout, all of a sudden that pain in my back shot up to a pain level of 10. I didn't know what had happened, but everything changed. As much as I hated to do it, I had to drop out of the gym. I was taking Tylenol around the clock with no relief. This was a terrible way to live. One day in May, I told my wife I thought I needed to go to the emergency room. When we were finally able to get in, they did some X-rays to see if I had broken something. Nothing was broken so they said all they could do was give me a shot of morphine for the pain and they sent me home. You know I had seen all these movies where they give someone morphine and they were immediately out of pain. Well, for me there wasn't even the least bit of help. He did get me an appointment with a neurologist in July, which meant I had two months of living with this pain just to get in to see the doctor. In the meantime, my life on earth was a living hell. Day in and day out for sixteen to eighteen hours a day I lay in bed hurting and wishing for an end to all this. There was even one night when June and the boys were gone that I kept looking at all those pills and thinking *I could end all this,* but in the end, I remembered the promise I had made all my family in Tomball while they were all standing around my bed. This was before I could talk. They were begging me not to give up; especially Jacob who just kept saying, "Dad, you just can't give up" over and over. I shook my head. Yes, thank goodness for that memory.

About this time, I was also really depressed about the way I looked. Probably because of all the medicine I was on, my skin had become so flakey. It was so bad I quit wearing anything dark so I couldn't see all those flakes. I only wore light grey or silver, which just made me look even more pale. I had also lost so much weight and muscle. June kept telling me how none of this mattered and it would get better, but you can tell someone this over and over and it still doesn't sink in. Also about this time, I rode with June to the grocery store one day, where she saw one of my customers and friends and she told him I was out in the truck. When he came out to see me, the first thing he said was, "Man you need to get out in the sun." I know he didn't mean anything by that, but to me it said a lot. I started seeing how bad I looked compared to just a few months ago.

There were two events coming up that I was dreading going to. The first was my daughter's birthday on July 29. The year before we'd had it at our house and I had such a good time playing with all the kids. It was the last time I had been with all the family before my heart attack, and I had enjoyed it so much. The other thing was having a family picture taken. Lindy and Melissa had given us a certificate to have one made of our whole family. I was really dreading this. For one thing it was August and really hot, the other was that I was going to have to be pushed around in a wheelchair. Luckily, on the day of the picture, we had one of the coolest days you could have in August in Texas. It was really cloudy with a wind blowing. Although I hurt, I was able to smile for most of the pictures.

Fast forward a couple of months, it was now getting close to Thanksgiving and Christmas, which were my favorite holidays. One because I had a few days off and two because I loved getting together with our large family. By large, I mean my mom and dad, their seven children, and their families, which included thirty-two grandchildren and already many great grandchildren. I was a person who always made a point to try to play and visit with all the kids! As the kids were all growing up, our family get-togethers were usually in Mom and Dad's backyard. I was always ready to play with the kids and then play forty-two in dominoes with my brothers, my mom, and even with my grandmother. We always played fun games and made so many great memories. But, now I was actually dreading my favorite things. I knew how bad I was going to be hurting, and dreaded hearing everyone telling me how great I looked, when in my mind I was thinking, *Oh sure.* While everyone was having a good time, I'd eat and then have to go lie down. Wow, lots of fun, right.

At this point, I was really getting aggravated with my life. I felt like a total failure. All my progress had been wiped out again. By now, I was in deep depression. First, I blamed my wife for saving me. I would go for days at a time and not talk. I would tell her I forgave her for saving me, but then something else would happen and I'd get mad at her again. I know I made her life miserable and I hate that.

I felt like I was stuck in the movie, *Groundhog Day,* with Bill Murray. Day in and day out, that's where I am and it was a terrible way to live! I know I have really hurt June's feelings and I have apologized so many times. She's told me over and over that all she needs is my love. It seemed like we would snap back at each other more and more, which was something we had never done before. Our sons would get upset too, because they had never seen us like this before. Several times I would call them in and apologize to them for making such a big deal out of nothing. I'd ask myself, what had happened to the family that I loved?

Then, sad to say, I blamed God for doing this to me. I would be so mad sometimes that I threw things across the living room. After all, I would think, look what He has taken from me: my family, my shop, my running, fishing, dove hunting, etc. You'll never know what it is like to go from talking to forty or fifty friends a day to none just like that. I wanted to know what I had done to deserve this. Then I wondered where the Jesus was who'd said in my dream, "I've got this, Steve!" I found myself asking bitterly, "Well, Jesus, why don't you have this?" What a terrible way for me to be! My wife wouldn't say much, but she would keep putting daily devotionals or a scripture reading by my chair. Eventually I would pick one up and say, "Oh yes, sure." Slowly though I would read and say "I can see this" or "This one does apply to me."

21

The Neurologist

I finally got an appointment with the neurologist sometime around the middle of June. The first thing she ordered was an MRI of my lower back. When she got the results of the MRI, she said it looked like I had a bulging disc at my L4 vertebra. She asked if I had ever fallen and I told her about when I had fallen and hit my tailbone. She then made me an appointment for the following week with pain management and wanted me to see a neurosurgeon. Just hearing her say the words *back surgery* terrified us. The following week at pain management, the doctor said they were going to do a spinal injection on my L3, L4, and L5 vertebras. First, I had to crawl up on and table and turn facedown, which was very hard for me. I had not been able to sleep any way but on my back since the surgery. I couldn't even sleep on my side because it hurt too much. It took me several minutes before I finally got upside down. There was a beautiful picture of a lake and some mountains on the wall, so I tried to focus on that. The first shot he gave me wasn't too bad, but then he said, "Now, you will feel this one," and man did I ever.

When we left, he said it would take five to seven days before it would kick in. Finally, some hope. About the fifth day around 2:00 pm all of a sudden, I had no pain. My wife was buying groceries. I called and told her it worked. I went right away and took a good hot shower letting the hot water run all over me for a long time. That felt so good.

When June got home, she and the boys were so happy to see me smiling again. June had been rubbing my back and legs with Bio Freeze every night trying to ease my pain. Sometimes she would get hand cramps from rubbing so hard. Maybe there would be an end to this. As fast as the pain relief came on, it went away just as fast. Again, we were all knocked to the bottom.

A few weeks later the doctors said that since I did get some relief they would try again. Once again, I had my hopes up so high. The wait was the worst thing. I kept thinking, *Will it work this time?* Once again, the pain went away after five days, and just as quickly it came back the next day. I think I started crying. After talking to the doctor, he said they would try a different type of steroid. It was a week before Thanksgiving. By this time my body was so weak from months of not doing any exercise and I was totally worn out from pain.

By now, my mind couldn't even concentrate long enough to watch sports on TV. I had lost all my interest in them. Before this I had lived to watch the Dallas Cowboys, Houston Astros, or Houston Rocket games.

By my birthday in December, I was finally getting a little relief from the pain and once again, began getting my strength back. I was able to start exercising again. I started getting my hopes up again. We had my birthday party at our house with my kids and grandchildren. Things were really looking up again. Thank you, Jesus, for telling me "I've got this!" This gave me hope and something to hold on to.

22

2020

Once again, I was on my way up. I was doing great at physical therapy and making good progress. Around the first of February, the therapist put some weights on my ankles and had me start doing leg exercises. And again, that terrible pain hit me and went up and down my sciatic nerve. This time was even worse than all the other times. It was so bad my wife had to help me back to the car. When I called pain management, they said it had lasted about 2 ½ months and I can only get a shot every three months. So, they set my appointment for around March 20. Until then they gave me a prescription for Tylenol 3. To say the least, this didn't even put a dent in the pain.

The next thing we knew the COVID virus was going rampant. They shut hospitals down except for emergencies, which meant more waiting. What was I going to do? Finally, in the middle of April our hospital partially opened to allow just a few clinics to start functioning. I called my doctor and he said he could get me in the next week. I think this was the third day they had been open. You can imagine how lucky I felt to get in so fast. After I got the shot, I had to wait a period of time to see if I was going to have a reaction from it. Finally, it was clear nothing was going to happen. I had no adverse reaction to the shot, but I also didn't get any relief from that shot at all. Talk about getting knocked down to the floor. Reluctantly, I called the neurosurgeon. I couldn't get an appointment until August. This was a full three months away. How was

I going to make it? My days were worse than they had ever been. All I could do was lay there and hurt 24 hours a day. I kept calling the surgeon's office in case they had a cancellation and would you believe I was able to get in around June 10.

Once there, the doctor said that he could try and shave a little of the bulge down, but he also said he only gave it a 50 percent chance of really working. And again, the quickest he could get me into an operating room was July 26. Well, I thought, at least there was a glimmer of hope. Again, I began calling regularly to see if there were any cancellations and, believe it or not, I got an appointment for June 29. When we showed up for that appointment, the doctor said I needed to get a new MRI before he did the procedure and it would be July 12. I continued calling right away and did get an appointment on June 30. With the MRI out of the way, we were ready. The next week we got a call from the nurse and she said they had a cancellation and could get me into an operating room on July 7. I couldn't believe we got through all of this in just a couple of weeks. I know this was Jesus working with me, prompting me to keep calling and checking.

The only problem still left was getting the insurance approved by Monday morning. It was Friday, July 3, and we were scheduled to check in the hospital at 6:00 am Monday morning, but we still had no word from the insurance. Monday morning came and we were still waiting while they tried to get approval. Finally, around 11:00 am we got the green light and away I went. After a successful surgery and with 9 staples in my back, I was headed home. The doctor also prescribed me a medicine called Hydrocodone, enough to last about six weeks. Gosh, this helped so much. The pain meds did the job, so I was feeling great. I still could do no bending or lifting. The last thing I wanted to do was break one of those staples. In three weeks, I went back to get the staples out and the surgeon told me to start getting off the hydrocodone. At this point, I had about three weeks left and he gave me two more weeks' worth of pills. For one week I was to take two pills a day and for the next week I would be down to one pill a day. That sounded just great. I still was limited, but in three more weeks I could start doing anything I wanted.

The first week came and went with no problem; I was doing great. No pain whatsoever. From four pills a day down to two wasn't bad at all, but when I was supposed to go down to one a day, I thought I might as well just stop taking them all together. Man, did I really mess up. Quitting cold turkey is definitely not the way to do this. I had severe withdrawals with cold sweats, dizziness, shaking. It felt like my skin was crawling (I don't know how to describe the experience of withdrawal any better than that) but it wasn't pleasant at all. All of these symptoms were going on day and night.

I found out the further away from my hydrocodone I got that all that pain I had before was still there and now I was out of my pain medicine. Once again, I desperately called my pain management doctor and they said that since I had had back surgery and it was unsuccessful, I was eligible for a spinal cord stimulator or an SCS. This is a device that goes inside your spinal column. There are two stimulators about three inches long that were lowered on two wires right into my L3, L4, and L5 lumbar segments. A battery is placed under the skin in your hip area with all the wires below the skin. At first, they put the battery on the outside to see how it is going to work. Next, they drill a hole in your spine and implant the stimulators. For three weeks you can barely move. The implant rep programs the SCS as to where you should be. There is a ten-day trial period. There were two days that it actually worked for me, so they said they would go ahead and put mine in. The surgery went fine, and I now had six staples in my upper back and nine staples in my rear. I had to spend the night at the hospital and my wife picked me up the next day and we headed home. Talk about a rough ride home. If my wife turned too fast or hit a bump that jarring pain would come over me.

23

The Implant

O nce I got home, I was told to avoid what they called BLTs, which meant no bending, lifting or twisting for three weeks. After three weeks, we went back to get the staples removed and the doctor said everything looked good. He then told me no exercising until February 1. The SCS rep was there to turn my implant on and get it set to the right program. When we left, I said to June, "I sure won't miss this place." What the SCS does is send an electrical pulse through your sciatic nerve and that blocks out the nerve pain. It doesn't cure the pain; it just blocks it out.

I was totally exhausted when we got home and when I got out of the car, I started to get a wave of pain that overtook me. The implant was shocking me badly. Quickly I got the thing turned off and called the rep and told her what was going on. She said she would meet me in Snook the next day to check it out. She met us there and reprogrammed the SCS and I immediately felt better, and over the next week I was trying to fine-tune it and hone in on the right setting. Finally, I found it and was able to get some relief. *Thank you, Jesus!*

I was counting the days until I could start exercising again. On February 1, I started trying to exercise. The pain of just moving and light exercise was very hard to take. Slowly I started to be able to do a little more each day. We have an elliptical seated bike that my niece, Andi, had given me and this was really a good exercise. I was even able to go outside and sit for about fifteen minutes at first and then for twenty to forty minutes. Life was great! Of course, by 5:00 or 6:00 in the afternoon, my body was entirely worn out and I was ready for bed. But at least I felt like I was getting better.

By April, I was once again walking with a cane and was able to do almost three quarters of a mile walking inside our house. I was even able to start driving a little again. I just knew this SCS was the answer I had been looking for.

On April 30, I had a procedure called Botox on my leg. This had been an ongoing treatment where my neurologist would inject certain muscles and ligaments with Botox to try to correct the inward turning of my foot. This is done gradually over many different sessions. This first procedure was done on a Friday and had to be done with me on my stomach. Once at home I was completely worn out and on Saturday morning when I got up my old familiar pain was back. I was really upset by this turn of events and wondered, *What is going on now?* I had to wait until Monday to call the rep. When I called her, she told me to move the setting on the SCS controller back to where she had originally put it. I did that and now I was getting a real shock up and down my sciatic nerve. It hurt so bad, but I left it there like she said. By Sunday, I was hurting so bad that I texted her and told her how bad I was hurting. When she called back, she sounded really aggravated that I had texted her on a Sunday. She made my wife and me feel like we were real dummies for not understanding what she was telling us to do. In other words, "don't bother me again" was the impression we both got from that conversation.

What followed was a living nightmare. I was back to hurting sixteen to eighteen hours a day. Again, I was counting the minutes until I could take my pain and sleep meds. It got so bad I had to call my primary doctor to see about getting back on Hydrocodone. This helped a little, but it truthfully wasn't doing much good, but I took it anyway just in case it might give me a little relief.

Once again, I was missing my wife's birthday, Mother's Day, and other family get-togethers. This was when I went through some of my darkest moments.

24

My Dad's Gift

In the past, our family had always had a family reunion at Thunderbird Resort on Lake Buchanan in June. There we would rent four or five large cabins and have a weekend of fun and visiting. They had basketball courts, volleyball net, horseshoes, a large swimming pool, a nice marina and the lake. There was something for everyone to enjoy, plus lots of good eats and visiting with each other. We thought it was the perfect place for our large family to get to spend time together. We went for around thirteen or fourteen straight years and what a great time we always had there.

My dad, my brother Dick and I would always be the first ones up around 5:00–5:30 in the morning. We would pull up our lawn chairs and sit there visiting enjoying the beauty of the lake and canyon, the quietness, and watch the sun coming up. We would always drink coffee and, since my cabin was the closest, I would go and get my dad his refills of coffee. What a great memory this was for me.

In June 2019, I had a dream that my dad and I were there drinking coffee just as we had done for so many years. You see in March 2018, just a few months before my heart attack, my dad had passed away. I shared this story with my family and most of them said they had never had a dream like this. I felt really blessed to have had it.

In June 2020 once again I had another dream. Jacob, John, and I were in Dad's old red and white truck and even though it had been sold years ago, we had it at the shop and all cleaned up just as my dad always kept it. He even opened up the hood and wiped off all the hoses and everything he could see. His wheels and the inside were cleaned every week. Even if it had just sat in his drive way, he still cleaned it anyway. Anyway, in this dream we went to eat at a steak house in Somerville called the Cottage Inn. They were famous for their huge steaks, hamburgers, and fish plates. Many Aggies made their way to Somerville just to get a steak. These steaks literally wouldn't fit on the plate. The boys and I were just coming out of the restaurant and getting into the truck when I looked across the street and saw my dad coming out the side door of another restaurant. He was dressed just as he usually did in his blue canvas tennis shoes, matching blue socks, and beige pants with a blue shirt. He started across the street and I said, "Look boys, there's Pawpaw." We got out of the truck and I could tell by the way he was walking he was on a mission. All my brothers and sister will tell you that when our dad had something to do, or on his mind, this is exactly the way he walked. As he got to us, John said, "Hi, Pawpaw!" and Dad reached out his hand and rubbed John's head and said, "Hi, Son" Then he stepped back and opened his arms to me wanting to give me a hug. I stepped up and he embraced me, patting my back four times. Then he stepped back, raising his arms to the sky, he shouted "The Lord is good, the Lord is good." The next morning, I started calling my brothers and sisters and my mom, telling them about my dream. Each time I told the story of that dream I would get emotional.

Earlier that month I had told June that if I was going to hurt just sitting around, I might as well hurt exercising. I got on the bike and started saying the Rosary. That is when it hit me that this was not just a dream of my dad, it was his way of coming to me to ease my conscience. Your see back in March, my dad, who was eighty-seven and had lots of health issues and heart problems, had been in the hospital and the doctors wanted to do more testing and he said no more tests or procedures. He told them he was ready to go to heaven. He was placed with Hospice and died three days later.

Like I told before, I had let my shop take precedence over my family. The rest of my siblings were there taking turns spending time with dad, but I could only go and visit a little while after five when I closed the shop. On Saturdays I could go for a while after we closed at noon and on Sundays, I could stay longer but I needed to leave by 10:00 pm because I had to get up at 5:00 to start my week. Eventually they moved Dad to the Hospice facility and still I didn't close the shop to spend as much time with him as my siblings. I went so far as to tell my brother Eddie to be sure and call me when it was getting close. *What a son!* When Eddie called at the end, I got there but Dad was already gone, so I never got to speak to him. At the funeral, we sat on the front row and I was the only one who really lost it. My brothers and I and our three brothers-in-law were Dad's pall bearers, plus Jacob and John because they were his special ones. After Mass as we started out of the church, but before we made it out the door of the church, I completely broke down. My mom had to get me by the hand and say "Steve, you have to finish this!" I think I took this harder than the rest because I didn't have closure like they did. I felt deep down that what I had done was wrong. I really beat myself up inside for not closing the shop. After this dream, I thought Dad had given me the gift of easing my pain. Something my dad had always done was pray the Rosary every day, so I made a promise that I would say the Rosary every day in his memory.

25

Falling Down a Deep Well

O ver the next several months, my pain got worse and worse. Finally, one day I told my wife and family that I had lost my will to live. This is when I went through my darkest times. One day my wife went for an early morning walk to do her praying and to spend a little time with God. As she walked, she was taking pictures here and there randomly on her phone. A couple of days later, as she was looking at those pictures, she came upon one taken by one of our tanks. Close to the water and just in the brush was a picture of a green orb. It really stood out. She showed it to me and I thought it looked like a green kid's ball. Then I made it bigger and I thought maybe it was a horse apple. She told me she would walk back up there if she could see it again, but there was nothing there. Later she showed it to her sister-in-law, Jane, and she sent this to us: "A green orb can carry a message of need for healing. This can be spiritual, emotional, mental, or physical healing. Another possible meaning is that the Spirit is there to deliver a healing to the individual." Is that neat or what. June and I were both needing help at that time to deal with all of this. June sent this picture to both of our families.

Where we lived before was a long way out of the way for anyone to come visit and we didn't get many visitors; now I was having visits from everyone. They were all sending me pictures of our family throughout the years. Many prayers were going up for me. They found a Christian counselor for me to go to in

College Station, and he helped me so much. When I first went, I was skeptical but he did a great job. He gave me a book about suffering called *Suffering: Gospel Hope when Life Doesn't Make Sense,* by Paul David Tripp. This book helped me see that I wasn't all alone and gave me hope again.

Around the end of July, I called my pain management doctor to see about a different type of procedure I had heard of and didn't think this doctor did. Then I decided to consult with an outside doctor about it. That doctor said he would have to look at all my records first. Shortly after this the PA called and said this was not what I needed and that I needed to contact the implant rep and get them to reprogram my implant. That's when I told her we were led to believe there weren't any more programs. That same day I got a call and yes, they could meet me the next day to get me reprogramed. I was so mad; I about blew my head off—all this time of hurting and to now find out there were more programs. My hopes were again high.

I decided to write a letter to that rep and give it to her when we met with her. I told all about how we had all suffered during this time, and about losing my will to live. I planned to give it to her the next day and had it in my pocket, but June totally refused to let me do that. Once in the room, I had to hold my tongue. I was furious and I know she felt it. June and I could both tell by the way she was acting that we thought the doctor had really gotten tough on her. So, I guess she didn't need that letter.

Adding to the stress on my wife at this time was the fact that her ninety-three-year-old father had been really sick and had died in March. Again, I felt as if I had let my family, and especially my wife, down because I didn't try to go to the funeral. I just knew I couldn't sit but a few minutes without hurting. I apologized to all her family for not trying and everyone seemed to understand. Then came the fact that we were going to be moving to her dad's home in Cooks Point. We had lived in our home for thirty-seven years. All I could do was keep thinking about all the wonderful memories I had in that house. It was going to be so hard to leave it.

June decided to totally remodel her dad's house. It had been built in the '70s and had very dark paneling. She redid both bathrooms, adding a walk-in shower in the master bath for me. She was doing all this while having to deal with me adding to her stress.

While all this was going on, the two new programs they had changed on my SCS didn't faze my pain. Somewhere around the first of August, I had had enough and begged my wife to just let me go. Crying, she said okay and we would call the doctor tomorrow. When we called, the doctor said, "Well, let us try again to get your pain under control and also work on your depression and start you on some new medicine." This was on a Thursday and I was at the end of my rope.

On Sunday, out of the blue, my mom called and wanted to know if she and my sister, Kristi, and her husband, could bring me Holy Communion. My mom had been a Eucharist Minister at St. Joseph's Hospital. I said yes and they drove out. After giving me Communion, they each took turns giving me their wise words, their scripture readings, and much more encouragement to keep on fighting. After lunch I went to my room and while lying in bed and it came to me, "Who am I to beg for a merciful end to this life, when Jesus endured what He went through for all of us." Later that afternoon, I called all of them to my room and told them they had just saved my life both spiritually and mentally. From that time on I knew that God was with me and that I could endure whatever I needed to.

26

The Call

O n Wednesday, August 18, I called my SCS rep and told her I had been on the level she told me to stay on and that I had been at a pain level of 10 for twelve hours. It had not helped at all. I asked her, "Was this normal?" She told me to go to the other program. Two days later, I texted her at 6:15 am because I was hurting so bad. I needed help and I needed it right away. I asked if she would please call ASAP. She never called. So I waited until 11:00 and I texted her again asking her to please text me what to do. Still no call. At 11:30 I texted again and apologized for texting so early but told her I had been in severe pain this whole week. Finally, I got a call and she just told me, "If this isn't working, have your wife take you to the emergency room." I told her they won't do anything and she replied, "Well, that is what you need to do" and hung up. I looked at my wife and said, "This is serious!" But here's the amazing call that probably saved my life.

Then, one morning, I was in my recliner around 3:00 am when it came to me to call my pain management doctor because I didn't have an appointment until September 6 for my next injection. That morning first thing, I called to find out what kind of shot they were going to give me. As God wanted, a new PA called me back and I told him what kind of trouble I was in and the I wanted to know what kind of shot they were planning to give me. He said, "Let me pull up your records and see." He said, "I see you have had five injections but it doesn't look like they worked very well." After a few minutes, he came back and said, "We are going to try a shot that targets the actual sciatic nerve." I then told him how severe the pain I was in was and that I didn't think I could make it until September 6. I told him that I had lost over ten pounds and was having to go to the bathroom sometimes two or three times an hour due to the pain. I told him I was on the cancellation list, but they had never called me. He said he would see what he could do. After a few minutes he said "How does next Monday sound?" I thanked him and told him he had probably just saved my life. Who else but God put that thought into my head to call then and who else had that new PA answer the call and really go look at my records? Who else but God let there be a cancellation that next Monday?

By Saturday, after the intense pain that I had been in for the last three weeks, I could literally feel my life slipping away. It felt like things were starting to shut down. I was so weak that I was having a hard time even getting up out of bed. I was even eating my meals in bed.

You can't imagine how much pain I was in when we got to the hospital Monday morning. Once in the room, the PA came in and went over all I had tried and been through. She said she was so sorry I had had so much to go through, and she was going to assign me to the boss over this program. From now on I would deal with the regional boss. As she was leaving my room, she ran into that regional boss and brought her in to meet me. She had me repeat my story of the nightmare I had had the last four months. She was looking at me the whole time and I could see the hurt in her eyes. She made an appointment for us to get reprogrammed on that Friday. After getting reprogrammed, I waited and waited for some relief. The shot I got did help some, but not enough.

27

A Jolt from Heaven

On September 9, I was still hurting badly and I was at a pain rating of 7–8. I was sitting up that morning around 3:00 am, when all of a sudden, I was hit with what felt like lightening going up and down my spine. The pain was off the chart. As I sat there a voice in my head told me, "Steve, turn that thing off. That's what has been hurting you." Then God spoke to me and said He wanted me to do what I do best and that is to write my stories. Well, I have always liked to write. In the sixth grade, I won a contest in Arlington with an essay about What America Meant to Me. All through school and college I liked to write papers. Over the last two years I was able to put together a series of stories that I had told my four kids over the years. Now all my grandchildren wanted me to tell those same stories over and over to them. I even made a cassette recording for them to listen to, but they still wanted me to tell them again and again. So, I decided to write them down and had Melissa make four sets of copies and put them in a folder with each one of my grandkids' names on it. I told her I wanted her to keep these until each of them had their first baby shower and to give them their folder so that my great grandchildren would know who I was and something about my life.

The next day was one of the most incredible days of my life. God was pouring into my heart and mind. Every thought that I had was about and for God. I can honestly say I've never experienced anything like this in my life. The feelings I had were so awesome.

I texted all my family and told them about my experience and that the first story God wanted me to write was a story about family, not just any family, but our family. I went back over all my photos and videos from the last three years. I saw the family singing at the ICU; I saw my first steps; I saw Larry shaving me and Theresa shampooing and giving me a haircut; I saw my nieces Madison and Whitney giving me a manicure and pedicure. The only picture I didn't have was one of when I woke up that day and saw my brothers Larry and Eddie each giving me a foot massage because the therapist said that would help wake up the nerves and muscles. Each one who came to visit would rub my arms, legs, and feet just trying to help. I ask you, is this a true family or what? I then thought of all my brother and sisters-in-law and how much help they have been to us. Connie and Randy, Rob and Jane, and Judy and Eddie, have all been wonderful to pitch in whenever June needed help with anything; whether it's working cows, fixing doorknobs, or replacing our septic system, they all have been here to help. I am so thankful for each of them.

Then I watched videos from my huge benefit that they all worked so hard to make such as success. This would have been my fortieth year in business for myself, and I have had thousands of employees. Of those, about 70-75 percent could say they had a happy childhood, and about 35-40 percent said they never get together with their families. They were always amazed that a family like ours could actually get together and enjoy it. Our mom and dad raised us to know what God, family, and love meant. That is not to say that there aren't times when we don't all agree on something, or get our feelings hurt, but it doesn't last long. In the end we are still family and our love is deep and lasting.

28

One Man's Prayer

My Dear Lord,

What a story you have given me over the last three years. You have guided me to the highest peaks and helped me through the lowest valleys. When you gave June that Chinese fortune cookie that said "You will soon witness a miracle," you didn't say how soon it would be. The miracle wasn't the fact that I was in such good shape that I survived the heart attack. You see that kind of stuff on TV all the time: "Man survives shark attack" or "Family barely survives flood."

No, Lord, the miracle was showing your people the power and the way you play a part in every one of our lives. When I was at my very lowest place, even begging for your mercy, you brought me life through Holy Communion. You took me almost to the bottom end and by your grace, you helped me make that call that saved my life. Now, that is the true miracle.

I thank you Lord. In all that I have been through, you don't know how blessed I am to have the family that I have. June has done everything and then some to try to make my life comfortable as possible. Some Dads can't brag enough about their children, but this dad can. Our daughters have both been such a huge help to us through all this. We were doubly blessed with Jacob and John who were probably stronger than any of us, helping in every way they could with all their trips to get ice packs for me; most of the time with a smile on their faces. Thank you, Lord, for the rest of my family for being loyal to come and visit me and give me encouraging words.

I am thankful to have been allowed through this experience to see the power and love that God has for His people. The ones I feel sorry for are those who don't have God on their side to help them when they need help.

Your Servant for Life,

Steve

29

"Lord, What Is My Purpose?"

I found myself asking, *What do you want me to do, Lord?* For three years now I have been beating myself up about what is God's reason for keeping me around. One night around 3:00 am, I couldn't sleep because of what I had endured in recent weeks. My brain and body were completely drained. It came to me in my thoughts that God didn't leave me here to give my story to churches as I had envisioned. He didn't want me to start any missions to help people who needed a friend, or who just needed someone to talk to. He didn't mean for me to mentor other people who were in pain. What He did want was to show others the power and the love that He has for His people.

I don't think many people can say they have had the opportunity to experience God's presence as many times as I have in my life. At eight different times in my life, I have interacted with Him. The first time was the train wreck in which I promised to be His servant for life. The second was the truck accident where six inches made all the difference between life or death. The third was my heart attack, where Jesus came and told me, "Steve, I've got this." The fourth was when He allowed my dad to come to me two years in a row to ease my conscience. Through Holy Communion, He let me see my mistakes. The last was when He brought me almost to the end and then guided me to make that call that saved my life. All of this was to show everyone the power He holds for all His people. All the time it was there right under my nose and I just couldn't see it. And now a seventh and eighth time when God completely entered my heart, mind, and soul with His thoughts. If this is what heaven is like, I know why this is every Christian's goal.

30

God Sends a Local Angel

A few months later, my wife took our dog to the vet for a snake bite on her leg. There in the waiting room was a lady we know from church who had brought her dog in also. They started talking and she asked June how I was doing. June told her about all the tough times I had been having, and the lady gave her number to June and said to give it to me and if I ever needed to talk that she would love to talk to me. You see, when she was in seventh grade, she was a cheerleader. One day she got dropped really hard and the result was a very tough time of healing. I think she is in her forties now. She has been dealing with this for a long time.

When she came home, June told me about her and gave me her number. It was a couple of weeks later that I decided to call her because I was really hurting at that time. We talked for about two hours. You can't believe how good it felt to have someone who understood what I had been through. Her name is Lori Oliverez. I was a friend of her step dad when I worked in the oil field. He was a big, strong man. He used to come in my shop and play basketball with us.

Lori told me about her over twenty years of suffering, what a terrible time she had dealing with her pain, and all the times she had to miss doing things with her family because she felt too bad to go anywhere. We shared about the terrible time we had dealing with the pain medicine and the hard time we both had trying to get off them. The withdrawal effects were so bad. We both said we couldn't imagine how hard it must be for someone who had been abusing drugs for years to quit. We shared about how we both felt like we were a weight holding our families back from going places and the guilty feelings we had when they had to stay home because of us.

She told me she had been through nine surgeries between 2011 and 2018. This made my three surgeries look like going to the doctor and getting stitches.

We both agreed that we often felt that other people thought we were weak because we couldn't just get off the pain killers. I know I told you earlier about how my self-image had suffered during this time and how I was very conscious of how people looked at me. Finally, I had found someone who knew exactly how I felt. I also told her of the shame I felt when I told my family that I had lost my will to live and about the time that I was going to text all my family that I had run my race the best I could, and how devastating this was to my kids, especially my sons who had to watch me trying to die. That's when she shared that she had been in that same situation several times. We both talked about how we had begged God for mercy, to please take us away from this misery. Just having her to talk to has helped me so much and that is why I call her my local angel. She also said that I was her angel and that God had done this for both of us. She also told me that whenever I needed someone to talk to, she will be there for me. I have called her several times to tell her or ask something about things that I was feeling. The latest was trying to get off an antidepressant. I found the side effects were much worse than getting off pain meds. One day I was hurting so bad and she comforted me with her words of encouragement by telling me to just keep praying and that I would get through this. Anyone else could tell me that, but hearing this from her made a huge difference.

One week I got a new walker and sent Lori and all my family a picture of my new wheels. I even left the tag on it calling it my dealer tags. It just felt good to give everyone something to smile about. I also started wearing brighter shirts instead of those grey or silver shirts. I was just doing small things to help my attitude, but it was all a step in the right direction.

The help that Lori has given me is unsurmountable. God knew that we both needed this and for that, I do thank Him. She also told me that she had turned all this over to God in 2018 and what fulfillment this has brought her.

31

Another Visit from Our Lord

On September 23, June and the boys were gone to Bryan to doctor appointments. That morning about 10:00 I was lying in bed when all at once God came to visit me. That whole day was nothing but feeling God's love and feeling how much He understands what I am going through. He reminded me that He "had this" and not to worry. The feeling is one that is so hard to explain, but it is like a warmth that comes over me and just leaves me in such a relaxed state of mind. Of course, I shared this with my whole family.

I have found my perfect time with God is between 2:00 and 4:00 am. I get up and go to the living room and sit down and pray my Rosary and then sit there in the dark and just let Him come to me. He hasn't come since then or given me anything else to write, but I know when He is ready, once again He will let me know what story to write. Actually, this book may be all He wants me to write. Time will tell.

It is just amazing to me to see how all these events have changed me. All my life I have listened to country music and loved it, but now all I want to listen to is contemporary Christian music and I am listening to a Bible study of both the Old and New Testaments. It's remarkable how an experience like this can change your whole life.

32

Lessons I Have Learned from This

That last visit from God made me realize that there wasn't any need of being mad at the doctors as one thing after another failed. There wasn't any need to be mad at that SCS rep who didn't help me. What God told me is this: *This is the road that I gave you to travel, travel it the best that you can, and know that I am on this journey with you and that there is nothing you can't go through with me at your side.* Everything that happened was the way God planned it, and understanding this really put my mind at ease. What a comfort this has been to me.

I found out one thing while researching my pain. You see even though I turned my implant off that night, God put lightning bolts up and down my spine. I was and still am getting shocked. This is called pseudo failure SCS, and many people have experienced this. It usually lasts for two to four months and after that, I should be able to turn it back on and start getting more relief.

Once again, learning this is God's plan for me; I fully and gratefully accept this. Being Catholic, I offer my pain for the poor souls in purgatory, so that someone may get to heaven sooner because of my suffering. So, I urge all of you if you are going through a really tough time in your life, just remember what Jesus endured on His way to the cross. Understanding this does help you and maybe it will ease your pain a little bit.

I have a friend who retired several year ago from the drug task force. What was so ironic about this is that his brother had at one time had back surgery and got started on opioids for pain management. When it came time for him to get off of them, he got off them for a little while, but gave in and started taking them again. This went on for quite a long time until his doctor quit prescribing them. He would go from one doctor to another before they really started to look at the opioid crisis. Eventually he ran out of this drug and he went to the streets to get them from drug dealers. Before you knew it, he was buying stronger and more and more of them. He was spending all this money on them. As his money ran out, it got harder and harder for him to get his fix. One day, he had had enough and took a gun and ended his life. At the time, my friend just couldn't forgive his brother for this. Years later, when I was having such a hard time, he was able to see me and how hard it had been for me to deal with my own pain and my struggle to quit my pain medications and he told me that now he could see what his brother had gone through, and it helped him to put his mind at ease about what he had done.

My friend also told me about his lieutenant in the task force. One time after he retired, he got some kind of infection in his leg. The doctors wanted to take it off, but he refused. As a result, he was taking Hydrocodone. Eventually he had to take more and more and finally he couldn't get relief any more. They finally found him with a gunshot. This is why these drugs are so dangerous. If anyone reading this knows someone like this, please try and get them help before it is too late.

33

Proof of Heaven

June's brother, Rob, who is our neighbor and a retired, very successful cross-country and track coach. Rob was named coach of the year in Texas for at least one year and maybe more. He now has a cross-country training facility which is right next door to us. Every year Rob has many running camps, as well as a huge cross-country meet here. This year I got to see firsthand how huge of an event this is. In all he had around thirty to thirty-five teams come. They all park in the pasture below our house. This event is tons of work and raises a lot of money. One of the really awesome things about this meet is that 100 percent of the money Rob makes goes to his favorite charity named Zoe's Mission. He has been to Africa a couple of times with their missionary group. The goal of this mission is this: "If you give a kid a fish, he will eat for a day; but if you teach a kid to fish, he will eat for Life." I have chosen to give 100 percent of any profit this book makes to go to Zoe's Mission.

One day, Rob was cleaning out his office and clearing out all his old folders, magazines, and paperwork and he came across this book, *Proof of Heaven*, by neurosurgeon, Dr. Eben Alexander. He had no idea where the book came from, but I had told him about my first visit with God, so he didn't throw it away. When he saw it was from a neurosurgeon who was a nonbeliever in miracles, he decided to read it. Then he brought it over for me to read. This book was written by a doctor in Boston. Like most people in the medical profession he tends not to believe in miracles. Sure, they have all seen cases where a person comes back from being declared dead, but they look at it from a scientific point of view—something triggered them to comeback. Dr. Alexander admitted that he wasn't much of a Christian usually, only going to church on Easter and Christmas and a few other times during the year.

One Sunday morning, he woke up with a bad pain in his back. Not thinking much of it, he took a hot bath which didn't help much. His wife wanted to call 911 but he told her not to. You see, the last thing a doctor wants is to have to ride in an ambulance and go to the Emergency Room. After a short time, the pain was so extreme they did call an ambulance. At the ER they were unsure of what was wrong so they couldn't give him anything for his pain until after tests were run. His head was now pounding, and after doing a MRI, the doctors knew this was something serious. They needed to get a sample of his spinal fluid. He was now a wild man, his eyes were bulging, and his neck was swelling and no one person could hold him down. It took six people just to hold him down. He could hear some of the doctors who he knew talking. A couple of months earlier, he had gone to Israel. They knew what he had, E.coli and meningitis; the worst a person could get. Later that day, he slipped into a coma.

He then went on an incredible journey to the spiritual heavens. Once arriving he was met by a girl sitting on a butterfly wing. She was to be his guide. She didn't speak to him verbally, but in his mind, she guided him through beautiful green valleys, mountains, and other beautiful places. There were silvery shapes all around. He heard a constant beating sound that was so very calming. One day he was met by a beautiful silver orb. This orb didn't talk either, but he knew this was God. He understood His thoughts. Later his guide took him before the gates of heaven. Sadly, he was turned away.

On Saturday, the doctors met with his family and told them it was time to make a decision as he had been brain dead for three days. The family asked to wait until Sunday morning. That morning his sister wanted to go in and hold his hand. One of the family had sat and held his hand for the entire week. As she was holding his hand, his eyes suddenly opened up. He was awake again. The next weeks were filled with the most amazing dreams. The same kind of dreams I experienced once I awoke.

A couple of months later he was able to go home. One day he was sitting at the breakfast table. When he was a baby, he had been adopted and for years had been looking for his birth parents. Finally, he found them and they told him he had three siblings: one brother and two sisters. One sister had died a long time ago when she was very young. They sent him pictures and, as he sat there looking at the picture, he realized that his dead sister had been his guide. What a story.

Eben Alexander would also get these urges to get up at 2:00 or 3:00 am and write, just like my times with God. He then went on gathering stories of other near-death experiences.

One story he told was of a lady from Georgia who called to tell him about her daughter who was dying of breast cancer. She said one day her daughter had a dream that she was met by a man wearing a yellow fedora and a yellow shirt. The Mom said "That was exactly what your grandfather had been buried in" and he had come to her daughter telling her everything was going to be all right.

After I came out of my induced coma, I had so many dreams that were so unbelievable such as seeing a black ocean liner with gold lights, the slide show of my life, and the most awesome one of these was when Jesus came to me driving a souped-up car, looked me right in the eyes and said, "Steve, I've got this!"

There was one time a while later when I wondered if these dreams were just a result of all the drugs that they had me on.

But no, how could these be just dreams when He came to me every time I needed Him so badly. This was as true as it gets.

That book is what inspired me to write my story. If you know anyone who is in need of inspiration, this book, *Proof of Heaven,* by Eben Alexander is a wonderful book for them to read.

34

Scriptures from My Wife

A s I told you, there were several times when I was mad at
God. My wife would leave these and many, many more
scriptures and articles by my chair hoping I would read them.
Most of the time I would set them to the side, but later when
she wasn't around, I would pick them up and read them. After a
couple of times of reading these, I slowly got over being mad at
God and everyone else.

Most of these readings and prayers came from a daily devotional my wife was reading called: *Jesus Calling*, by Sarah Young.
The first said this:

> I am with you and for you when you decide on a
> course of action that is in line with my will, nothing
> on earth can stop you! You may encounter many
> obstacles as you move towards your goal, but don't
> be discouraged-never give up! With my help, you
> can overcome any obstacle. Do not expect an easy
> path as you journey hand and hand with me, but
> do remember that I am your ever-present helper!
> Omnipotent! Much, much stress results from
> wanting to make things happen before their time
> has come! One of the main ways I assert my sover-
> eignty is in the timing of events. If you want to stay
> close to me and do things my way, ask me to show

the path forward moment by moment instead of dashing headlong toward your goal. Let me set the pace! Slow down, enjoy being in my presence.

Be on guard against the pit of self-pity. When you are weary or not well, this demonic trap is the greatest danger you face. Don't even go near the edge of the pit. The edges crumble easily and before you know it, you are on your way down. It is ever so much harder to get out of the pit than to keep a safe distance from it. That is why I tell you to be on guard. There are several ways to protect yourself from self-pity. When you are occupied with praising and thinking of me, it is impossible to feel sorry for yourself. Also, the closer you live to me the more distance there is between you and the pit! Live in the light of my presence by fixing your eyes on me. Then you will be able to run with endurance the race I have set before you without stumbling or falling.

Something that I have found useful is that every time a thought of feeling sorry or a negative feeling enters my mind, I repeat this over and over and the thought will leave me: "Oh my Jesus, forgive my sins, save me from the fires of hell. Help lead my soul to heaven." At first, I would have to say this so many times but it would work.

I am convinced that these negative thoughts such as feeling sorry for myself, wanting mercy from my pain, are all works of the devil trying to get hold of my mind. By repeating this, it drove him from my mind. I know what a hold the devil had on me when I was at my lowest.

These were some of the scriptures June brought to me:

Consider it pure joy whenever you face trials of many kinds, because you know the testing of your faith develops perseverance. (James 1:2–3)

No discipline seems pleasant at the time, later on however it produces a harvest of righteousness and peace for those who have been trained for it. (Hebrews 12:11)

Our light and momentary problems are achieving for us eternal glory that far outweighs them all. (2 Corinthians 4:17)

35

The Book of Job

In the past thirty years, I think I have read the Book of Job maybe three times. I had so many of my customers and friends who would come in telling me about the troubles they were having in their lives. One man's wife had left him and cleaned out all of his money, which was a large amount. Then his son who lived in Houston had gotten hooked on drugs, and he was about at his wits' end. That's when I told him about the Book of Job. He had never really gone to church much and didn't know what I was talking about. About a month later, he came and told me that he'd read it and he wondered how any man could go through all of that and still have trust and love for God. We talked about an hour and when he left, he didn't feel quite so bad.

Another time that really landed close to home for me was when we had first moved to Somerville. One of the first couples we met were Ricky and Connie Mantey. Connie and I had grown up in the same neighborhood. She even baby sat for Jacob and John for a couple of years. It turned out she was related to June. At the time Ricky and Connie had a catering business and eventually opened a restaurant. I often ate lunch there several times a week. Connie would come and sit down and visit with me all the time. One year, her son, Ricky, who was a firefighter in Bryan, was hurt in a fire at the Knights of Columbus ballroom. He was severely burned and was taken to the burn center in Galveston. She stayed down there with him. One day she came home and was at the restaurant when

I came in. She told me, "Steve I don't know if I can handle this." I gave her a big hug and told her it would be okay; the good Lord would take care of it. Eventually Ricky came home. Many years later, she came and sat down with me and started crying. I asked her what was wrong and she told me that her husband, Rick, had cancer. I sat there stunned and that's when I asked if she had ever read the Book of Job. She said she had heard of it, but had never really read it. I told her about all the tests God gave Job and how he never gave in and kept his love and faith in God. Rick eventually died and some days she would tell me, "I just can't keep going on." I'd tell her that she had to, not just for herself, but for her sons as well. Many years later her own health started failing and one day she had a stroke and passed on. This was very close to me because of how long I had known her. There is one thing for sure, she had earned her pass to heaven while on this earth, which should be the goal of every Christian.

I read the Book of Job when I was at St. Joseph's Rehab. I would talk to all the nurses that came in, telling my "Steve, I've got this" story. One of the nurses, named Carol, was so sweet and would stay and talk to me for long periods of time. Of course, I was at no loss of words, just desperate to keep talking to someone. It turned out she lived in Lyons where my shop was. Later when I started in physical training in Caldwell, my therapist's name was Mike and we got to talking one day. He knew where my shop was and had come in a few times. He also lived in Lyons. I said "Wow, there was a nurse who lived in Lyons who I got to know while there." He asked me what I thought of her. I told him how she took so much time to talk to me and then he told me that was his wife. We both got a good laugh out of that. I started telling him my story of meeting Jesus, and I came to find out that he could almost tell the whole story to me, because she had come home and told it to him.

36

Was This What God Wanted?

In early spring of 2020, June was out mowing while I lay in bed thinking. All of a sudden, I had an urge to write my story and share it with as many people as I could. Two nights before this I'd had a dream. I was still working and told my employees I was going to DQ to eat. When I got there, I saw three ladies from the bank, Beverly, Doris, and Carolyn, sitting at a long table at the back. I was friends with most of them, not just from the bank, but they were also customers of my shop. We made it our practice to go pick up their cars from the bank and take them to the shop and complete whatever the need was and then take the car back to the bank. We had provided this service for over twelve years, and most of the bank employees were good friends. Even though I was dressed in my dirty work clothes, the ladies invited me back and I sat with them and told them the whole story about Jesus coming to me. They were amazed and told me more people needed to hear that story. When my wife came in from mowing, I told her that I wanted to make as many copies as I could and mail one to all the churches in our area since I knew most of the pastors, priests and deacons around here. I told her I didn't care what it cost, but I wanted to put it in our local paper, *The Burleson County Tribune.* I was so excited, but she told me that you never see this kind of story in our paper.

So, I gave up on the newspaper idea and thought about my Facebook page "Steve's Race." I think when I first had my heart attack, I had over 1200 prayer warriors praying for me and keeping up with my progress on it. My daughter would type updates there and post them. But I knew the people who really needed to read my story wouldn't see it there.

About a week later, Pastor Vicki from First United Methodist Church called me and wanted to know if I would give my testimony to their congregation. I told her I would look forward to doing that, but first I had a back surgery coming up. I told her I would call as soon as I was able to do it. I was so looking forward to doing this as so many of that congregation were friends of mine. Sadly, after my surgery didn't help me, I told her that I just couldn't do it. This was again a big letdown for me. I just couldn't figure out why God gave me the inspiration to write my story, but I couldn't tell it like I thought I was supposed to do.

Around March, Pastor Vicki called me again to see how I was doing, but after an implant I had just started back to exercising and wasn't near strong enough to do it yet. I told her how much I wanted to. About a week later she called and asked me if I would tell my story over the phone to her congregation. This would be great. The next Sunday, she called me and I did tell my story to them. I just wish I could have done it face to face and visited with some of my friends who were there, but I wasn't able to do that then. We had planned to do another session called the "Pit Stop" and I would tell some of my other experiences, but, after my implant didn't work, I was in so much pain, I just wasn't able to do this.

Once again, this was another time of disappointment. This was during a time when I was at my lowest. Here God had given me a task to do which I did—I wrote the story—but yet I didn't get to tell it to others to help them. *Why?* I think now is the time He has chosen for me to share these experiences after teaching me so much. I think writing this book is what He wants me to do. Again, He keeps me busy giving me more to write.

37

Other Little Things

I am so fortunate to have so many family members who are so in touch with the Lord and have shared scriptures and visits to help me. During these difficult years, many members of my family and friends have shown me their love through their words of encouragement and acts of kindness. I would like to share just a few of these with you.

My three brothers, Larry, Dick and Eddie have been great about stopping by now and then for visits. Sometimes just fifteen minutes; sometimes, two hours. We would talk about how much fun we had during our childhood. We shared so many memories of growing up, getting into mischief, playing all kinds of games, and just having "boy fun" together. One thing Larry and I talked about was our times at St. Mary's Catholic School in Amarillo. We were both altar boys together, and Larry was much better at that than I was. At first, they put us on the same side of the altar and this sometimes led us to elbowing each other and then getting tickled. Then when they put us on opposite sides of the altar, we would start making faces at each other and start laughing. This was back in the '60s and our church was a solemn service, much of it in Latin. First, we got in trouble with the priest, and next we got in trouble when we got home. Each visit seemed to bring out a different memory and we would end up with a good laugh. All these little visits did so much for me and went a long way in helping me make it through another day.

On several occasions, my daughter Lindy sent me a daily devotional that she listens to on her way to work, where she has a very demanding job. If she heard one that she thought I might enjoy she would send it to me, and I always appreciated her taking the time to do that.

Now that we live at Cooks Point, my sister-in-law Connie lives on one side of us, and Rob, June's brother on the other side. They are both retired coaches. Connie is so good about inspiring me to keep pushing. Her visits several times a week are very helpful to keep me pushing myself. I call her my private cheerleader. Rob comes by for a visit a couple of times a week and just talking to him is motivation for me.

These are some of the scriptures and messages that I have received that have helped me so much.

From my daughter Melissa:

> *Three times I begged the Lord to take it away: each time he said "My grace is all you need. My power works best in weakness." So, I am proud to boast about my weaknesses so that the power of Christ can work thru me. For when I am weak, I am strong.* (2 Corinthians 12:8–10)

From my sister Cindy: "Thinking of you, Brother. I love you and admire your fight in this. I know it is not easy."

From my sister Kathy: "You two have been through so much the last three years. Know that we love both of you and will continue to pray for you. June, what can I say . . . true grit and tough as nails. So thankful Steve has you by his side. Continue to get stronger. You have always been a fighter!"

From my sister Kristi:

Hold firmly to the word of God. Then, on the day of Christ's return, I [Paul], will be proud I did not run the race in vain and that my work was not useless. But I will rejoice even if I lose my life pouring it out like a liquid offering to God. And I want all of you to share my Joy. (Philippians 2:16–17)

From my Mom: "My message for today is keep knocking on God's door. He will answer in His own time."

From Lori, my local angel: "We always find that those who walked closest to Christ were those who had to bear the greatest trials."—St. Teresa of Avila

From my sister-in-law Theresa: "God is saying to you today, 'I know you are going through a difficult time right now... and you are dealing with multiple circumstances and a lot of emotional pain. It seems as though before you can get through one thing, another thing happens. I don't always still the storm around you...sometimes I still the storm raging in you. Do not faint... I am strengthening you in areas that you cannot see right now. You and I will get through this together... like we always do.' Everything will be all right."

My sister-in Law Tammy: "And I am convinced that nothing can separate us from God's love. So, we can say with confidence, *The Lord is my helper, so I will have no fear of what people can do to me.* (Hebrews 13:6)."

From Melissa: "God wants more for your life even more than you do. Will you trust him? *Abba, Father, He cried out, everything is possible for you. Please take this cup of suffering away from me; yet, I want your will to be done, not mine* (Mark 14:36)."

Things I have prayed about the most, God has chosen not to remove, but like Job, I say, *though he slay me, yet will I hope in him* (Job 3:15).

An awesome sermon from Pastor Rick: "When God doesn't take the pain away." Suffering is the ladder to heaven. What a blessing He chose you to give this gift to. The Saints used to pray for hardship because they truly understood the meaning of this. Your story brought tears to my eyes. I am so proud of you and know that Jesus is saying, 'Well done, my servant!'"

I just want to thank each and every one of you who have encouraged and helped me make it this far!

38

The Gift above All Gifts!

As I have said before, I didn't know if God would ever come to me again as He had done two other times, but I got an answer on Christmas Eve this year.

Back around the first of December, my shot was wearing off and once again my pain level was high. I was so looking forward to having an enjoyable pain free Christmas with my family, but it wasn't looking as if that was going to happen. I called my pain management doctor to see if I could get in and get another shot before Christmas. They said the soonest would be December 30. They would put me on the list if there was a cancellation. Every night, I would pray that I could get in before Christmas, but the closer to Christmas it got, the more I knew they weren't going to call.

On Christmas Eve around 5:00 am, I was praying and inviting the Lord to come to me, when He did, just as He had done the other two times. Once again, I was filled with His love, His thoughts, and His warmth. I felt no pain at all until around 11:00 am. And just like before, He was gone, but not from my mind. I was so happy and excited that I told my whole family what I had experienced. This made my Christmas so much better than the previous three I had experienced.

Making it even more special was Christmas day when my sister, Kristi, texted me and told me that after coming to see me when our family celebrated Christmas together the previous week and I didn't feel like being there, my Mom, brother Eddie, Kristi and her husband, Kevin, and one of their sons had come to visit me at our home. This cheered me up so much to think they would take time out from the party to come visit me. When they were here, I told them all about my two previous visits from God and that as a Christian, if this is what heaven was like, I knew why we all strive to get there. Anyway, in her text, she told me that her son was so moved by my story that he had told one of his brothers that he was going to start making an effort to go back to church again. Do you know how awesome this made me feel?

Now you know why I was on cloud nine for our entire Christmas with all my family gathered around me. Yes, this was a "Gift above all gifts!"

39

A Word of Encouragement

In conclusion, I would like to ask anyone who is reading this book who knows someone who is going through a really tough time mentally, spiritually or physically, please share this book with them. I hope it will give them hope and encourages them to keep looking up to God. He is there and He is listening, and He will help in His own time. As in my case, it seems so slow, but I am content just knowing what my mission in life is. Believe me, it may not seem like God is listening which was my case, but when He came to me it woke me up to His power and love. May the peace of God be with each of you!